Best Practices in Replenishment of Forward Pick Locations

An Executive Briefing

By Jan Young

Best Practices in Replenishment of Forward Pick Locations

Jan B Young

Copyright © 2005 by Jan B Young
All Rights Reserved

ISBN 978-1-105-37944-4

Other Books From Jan Young Available at www.lulu.com

LOGISTICS

Choosing and Using a Consultant
 Finding a consultant who will actually be worth you time and money

Cycle Count and Physical Inventory Design and Execution
 Designing and operating efficient and effective methods

Designing and Using Carousels in the Warehouse
 Analyzing operations to design the optimum carousel installation

Selecting, Buying, Installing and Using a Modern Warehouse Management System
 The title says it all

Simulation in the Supply Chain
 What simulation technology can and cannot do in the supply chain

Supply Chain Metrics
 How to measure and monitor supply chain operations

FICTION

Mom and Me
 Three novellas prominently featuring cats

Claude
 A novel of the distant future

Eternity
 A life in heaven is not a bed of roses

TRAVEL

Northwest USA by RV
 Our 2010 travel to Oregon and Washington with lots of other stops, all in full color

Missouri and Maine by RV
 Two trips in 2009, one to Missouri and one to Maine in full color

Alaska by RV
 Our 2008 trip to Alaska, western Canada and the northwestern USA in full color

Atlantic Coast by RV
 2011 travel through Alabama to Georgia and the Carolinas

CARS AND TRAINS

Studebaker and the Railroads
 A two volume history of the Studebaker Corporation of South Bend, Indiana, railroading in the South Bend area, and connections between them

Tales of Studebaker: The Early Years
 Historic sidelights and illuminating stories about the company and the people

History of the American Automobile Industry
 Reprint of a 1916 history written by the editor of *The Automobile*, David Beecroft

The Studebaker History Corner
 More than a hundred short historic stories about Studebaker

Studebaker Bibliography
 A catalog of almost five thousand books and articles about Studebaker

History of the Studebaker Corporation
 Reprint of a rare 1918 book by Albert Erskine, Studebaker's President

TW and ASR Indexes
 Indexes of the content of Turning Wheels and Antique Studebaker Review magazines

The Life of Clement Studebaker
 Reprint of a biography believed to have been written by Ann Studebaker after his death

GENERAL INTEREST

State Flags of the United States
 Images, symbolism and history of the US state and territorial flags in color

The United States Constitution
 The history and content of the US Constitution and its amendments

Thirty Years as a Volunteer Treasurer
 What I learned as a church treasurer

Our Ancestry
 A three volume set listing almost twelve thousand people

The Assassins
 Forty-six historic stories of murder and mayhem on a global scale

Table of Contents

Introduction 1
Theory of Replenishment 4
Replenishment Cost 10
Item Replenishment Decisions 12
Replenishment Movement Generation and Control 17
Direct Put-Away 26
Replenishment With Highly Variable Demand 29
Cascading Replenishment 32
Summary 35

Introduction

Purpose of this Paper

Excellence in logistics is almost never the result of a masterstroke, but instead comes from the slow and patient accumulation of many small things, each done very well. This paper is about the elimination of wasted effort in the warehouse, and thus the improvement of productivity and the reduction of effort. There is no silver bullet.

The replenishment of forward picking locations is a thorn in the side of many warehouses. It contributes nothing directly to warehouse performance, but is nevertheless indispensable. When too much attention is paid to it, other important work suffers. When too little is paid, picking locations run dry and people waste hours dashing about the warehouse trying to find product. The proper management of forward picking locations and their replenishment can have significant impact and, therefore, deserves attention.

Experience in many warehouses has led us to believe that few warehouse managers think about the theory of replenishment and even fewer consider the right

Best Practices in Replenishment

tradeoffs when deciding how to handle new items and velocity changes in existing items.

When a new item arrives in the warehouse, there is a strong tendency in many businesses to simply assign it a forward picking location without detailed consideration of how it should be handled. The fact is that not all items should be picked from forward locations and that many replenishment moves are simply wasted effort. Forward pick locations in many warehouses are incorrectly sized, resulting in a costly and error prone replenishment operation.

Further, advanced warehouses that regularly reslot and adapt their layout to changing demand patterns often miss the mark because most commercially-available slotting systems simply assume that every item should have a forward picking location. In most businesses, that is certainly not the case.

This executive briefing reviews the theory of replenishment. It discusses when items should be replenished and when they should be picked directly from reserve stock. It further discusses the handling and management of multiple reserve locations and of multiple forward locations.

Best Practices in Replenishment

The use of cascading replenishment and the practice of wave replenishment to one-time locations are both covered. The result is a comprehensive review of the replenishment function that has the potential of both simplifying your operation and, at the same time, improving productivity.

About the Author

Jan Young is a trained Industrial Engineer with thirty-eight years experience in manufacturing and distribution. Now retired, he has:

- Managed a factory and a warehouse employing over a hundred workers in a 24/7/365 continuous operation

- Sold, installed, configured and maintained both manufacturing planning and warehouse management systems on a global scale for more than twenty-five years

- Designed a warehouse management system. That system, aimed at the top-tier market, was one of the premier, commercially-available systems when introduced

- Consulted in more than fifty warehouses in ten countries

Theory of Replenishment

The theory of replenishment is really quite simple.

Let's say we have 100 different products that arrive in the warehouse on pallets. Each pallet contains a different product and each holds 1,000 pieces of that product. The simplest possible arrangement is to just put these pallets on the floor and send the pickers out to fill orders.

The problem with simplicity is that the picking of an order for ten different items might require a travel pattern like the one shown by the dashed line in the drawing on the next page (Figure 1). On reflection, we can see that the picker has spent a great deal of time walking past product that he or she will not pick.

The pick path shown in Figure 1 is about 260 feet long. If the picker walks at 3 feet per second, travel time will be 87 seconds, or about 1.44 minutes. If the picker is paid $14 per hour and if we add 30% for benefits, the cost of the travel for this one order is about 44¢. Multiply that by the number of orders you ship in a year and increase it for the size of your warehouse

Best Practices in Replenishment

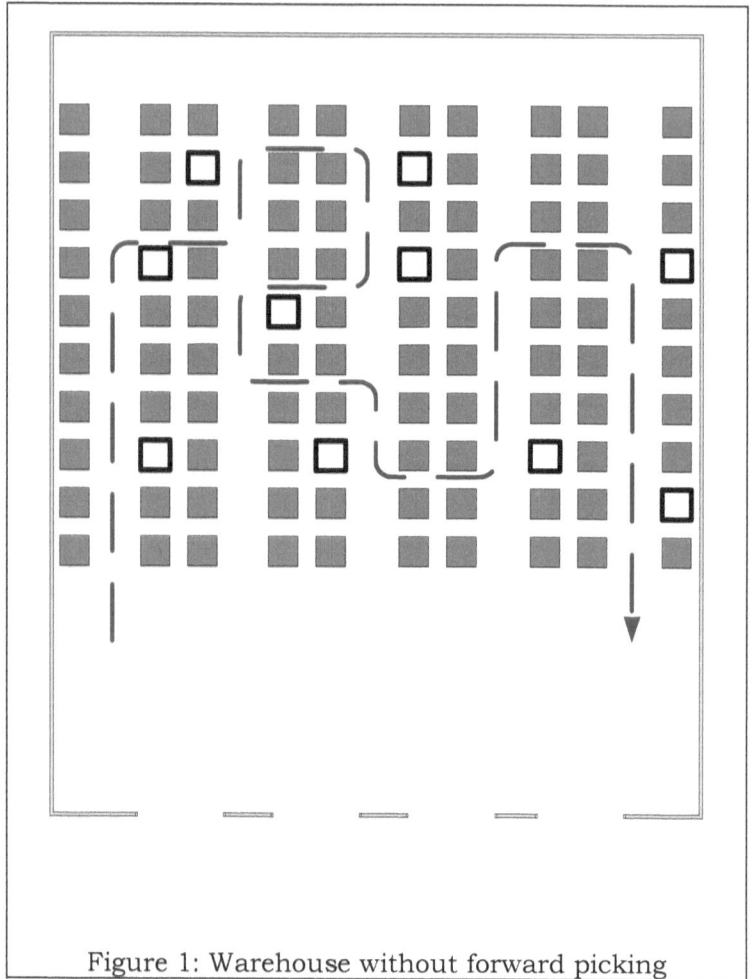

Figure 1: Warehouse without forward picking

(which is doubtlessly much larger), and the cost begins to become substantial.

Let's extend the example slightly.

If we allow five seconds for the picker to reach down, pick a single piece from a pallet, and make a tick mark on his pick sheet, then the total pick time was 50 seconds.

Add that to the travel time and we find that the order took 137 seconds or 2.28 minutes to complete. The hard part to swallow is that the picker spent 63% of his or her time walking and only 37% picking.

In fact, many sources say that pickers typically spend 70% of their time traveling. Although proof of this statistic is elusive, our example tends to justify it.

To reduce the travel distance and thus reduce cost, we need to get the product closer together. This can be done by setting up a small area in the front of the warehouse, stocking it with (for instance) ten pieces of each item, and eliminating the aisle space between the items. This space, which is of course, the forward pick zone, is shown crosshatched in Figure 2.

By forward picking these hundred items, we have reduced the pick path to 46 feet, cut the travel time to 15 seconds, cut the cost of travel to 8¢ and increased the ratio of pick time to total time from 37% to 77%.

Best Practices in Replenishment

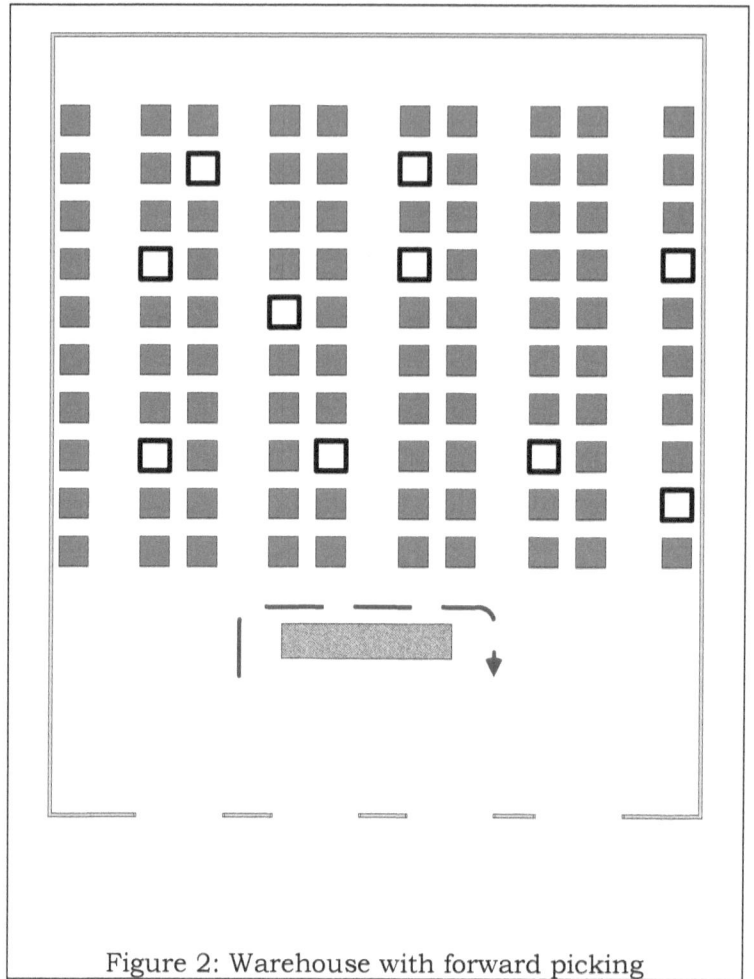

Figure 2: Warehouse with forward picking

So far, so good. Unfortunately, it isn't quite that easy. There is a cost to pay: If the forward pick location contains ten pieces of each product, then every tenth pick we have to send someone out into the

7

Best Practices in Replenishment

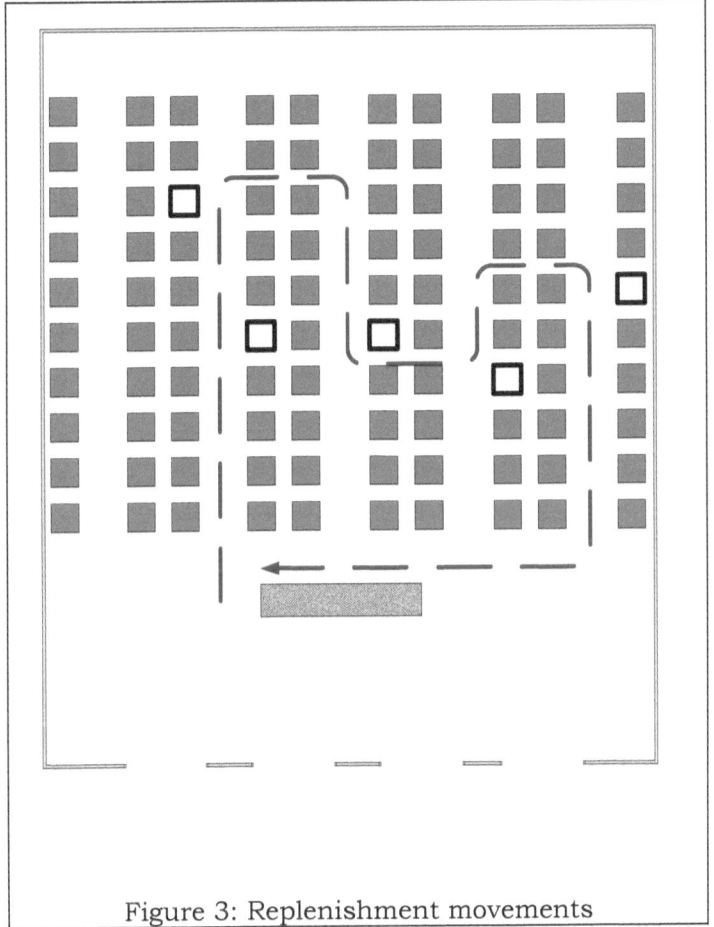

Figure 3: Replenishment movements

warehouse to move another ten pieces from reserve to forward. We call this work "replenishment."

For the sake of argument, let's say the replenisher can physically handle five replenishments at a time. The path length shown in Figure 3 is 212 feet. This equates to 71 seconds of travel and if we allow ten seconds for each pick (because the replenisher has to count out ten pieces), and five seconds for each putaway, the total time comes to 146 seconds or 2.4 minutes or 73¢. However, it only has to be done for every five orders, so the cost per order is 14.6¢. This compares favorably to the reduction we made from 44¢ to 8¢ by instituting the concept of replenishment.

Of course there are many variables including the distance between reserve and forward locations, the size of forward locations, the number of items that fit into them, the amount that a replenisher can handle in a single trip, and more. The reader may also detect the fact that the example shown above was cooked to make the numbers come out right. But the principle is illustrated.

Fundamentally, replenishment saves money by reducing picker travel. Travel is reduced by making pick locations smaller than reserve locations and by putting them closer together. This reduces the amount of unordered material the picker has to walk past. All of this is done at the cost of making replenishment movements.

Replenishment Cost

Most warehouses set up forward pick zones and do replenishment because it dramatically reduces travel distance and time for the pickers. Offsetting that savings, of course, is the cost of the replenishment activity itself. There are three costs that should be considered

First is the obvious cost of the people who do the replenishment work and the equipment they use. This cost is generally proportional to the amount of replenishment done.

Second, and less obvious, replenishment generally reduces our ability to efficiently utilize warehouse space by forcing us to subdivide the warehouse into picking and reserve areas. Every time we subdivide the physical layout of the warehouse, we pay a penalty in space utilization and in reduced storage flexibility because each warehouse area requires some amount of vacant space to provide working room and the more subdivisions we have, the more empty space we will need.

And third, replenishment creates a new job classification that requires training and supervision. The existence of this

Best Practices in Replenishment

classification (that of replenisher) creates overhead, makes the supervisor's job of assigning personnel more difficult, and tends to increase idle time. Much like space utilization, the more job classifications we have, the more idle time we tend to incur.

If a really detailed theoretical analysis were to be done, a few warehouses would find that replenishment is not justified at all while many would find that replenishment is justified only for some items and that other items are more economically picked directly from reserve.

Even if a warehouse is constrained by its current physical layout and by the vehicles and equipment currently in use, analysis should be done at least on a sampling of products to determine which should be replenished and in what quantities, and which should not. Once complete, this analysis can be refined, creating rules of thumb for use as new products are introduced and as volume changes occur for existing products. However, the most sophisticated (and efficient) warehouses will find ways to automate the analysis so it can be done in detail for all new products as they are introduced and for existing products on a regular recurring basis.

Best Practices in Replenishment

Item Replenishment Decisions

Essentially we have a choice for each item in the warehouse: we can pick small quantities from a replenished forward picking location, or we can skip the idea of forward picking and replenishment and do all picks, large and small, directly from reserve stock. Of course, we should do whichever is fastest and most cost-effective.

The complex part of this decision is the positioning of items in the warehouse. If we choose to replenish an item, we indirectly increase the size of the forward picking area and thus increase picker travel distances. This means (1) that all decisions to replenish or not replenish are interconnected in the overall productivity picture, and (2) that some items do not deserve forward picking locations even if it would shorten travel for them because their volume is so low or their bulk is so large that the added total travel overwhelms the savings for that one item.

Following this logic a little further, it means that some items should not be represented in the forward pick area and that the choice should be made based on physical item size and on pick volume.

Best Practices in Replenishment

Associated with the decision to replenish an item or not is the question of how large the item's forward pick location should be. Larger locations mean that replenishment quantities can be larger, so there can be fewer of them and they will be more efficient. Smaller pick locations, however, occupy less aisle space, tend to make the forward picking area smaller, and thus require less picker travel.

And finally, having decided that an item should be forward picked and that its location should be of a certain size, we need to decide where that pick location should be.

To truly optimize and achieve the maximum possible productivity, these decisions should be made intelligently and knowledgeably for every new item as it is introduced into the warehouse and then, depending on seasonality factors and on product life cycles, should be made again from time to time as product pick volumes change.

Commercially available slotting software generally does a very good job of determining where items should be placed in an existing forward pick zone and, when volume changes occur, it does a good job of specifying where they should be moved. How-

Best Practices in Replenishment

ever, there are drawbacks. First, few slotting systems will evaluate location sizes and recommend increases or decreases in existing racking. Second, to our knowledge, none will evaluate items to decide whether or not they should be forward picked and replenished at all. Third, none will recommend changes to the overall size of a forward pick zone[1]. And on top of those issues, many warehouses have not invested in slotting systems and therefore must make their replenishment and product placement decisions manually.

Because optimal replenishment is so dependent on warehouse layout, product size and velocities, vehicles in use, and other factors, there can be no specific formulae and only a few general observations can be made outside of the context of a specific site:

1. If a product is being replenished more often than once a day and if that replenishment frequency persists over a period of time, then the replenishment quantities are too small. Replenishment quantities are

---

[1] Note to slotting system suppliers: You can and should do better.

Best Practices in Replenishment

generally driven by the size of the forward pick location.

2. If a product is being replenished more often than every five picks, then the replenishment quantities are too small. (And in many businesses, the number five is too small.)

3. If a product is being replenished less often than once a month, the replenishment quantities and thus the forward pick location size are too big (unless the product itself is very small).

4. If product is replenished in a container or on a pallet and if the container or pallet is retained in the forward picking location, then the forward pick location must be large enough to hold at least two containers or pallets. The idea of picking from a pallet in the forward area and then replacing the pallet when it is picked empty simply does not work because there are always timing issues with removal of the empty pallet and its replacement with a full one. Pickers too often find themselves waiting for the replenishment.

Best Practices in Replenishment

5. No forward pick location should be larger than twice the amount a replenisher can carry in a single trip.

Despite the lack of simple rules, a competent warehouse engineer can and should look at the forward picking situation regularly to recommend product movement (using either software or manual methods), pick location size changes, and changes to the sizes of the forward pick zones. It is management's job to see that the proper people are tasked with this responsibility and that the work is accomplished.

Replenishment Movement Generation and Control

Efficient and effective replenishment, of course, is more than just deciding to do it and assigning locations. The product must be physically moved from reserve to forward picking in the right quantities at the right times. Failure to execute replenishments well will result in either or both of two problems:

1. If replenishments are done too soon or in too-large quantities, the operator will find that there isn't room in the forward picking location for the product. He or she will be faced either with returning part of the replenishment to the reserve location, or putting the replenishment somewhere else – often on the floor near the forward pick location – and then coming back later to finish the move. Regardless of which alternative is chosen, time and effort has been wasted.

2. If replenishments are done too late or in too-small quantities, pickers will run out of stock and will find themselves either skipping picks and coming back later to see if the

stock has been delivered, standing and waiting for the replenishment, or simply shorting the order. None of these alternatives is desirable.

System Generation of Replenishments

In businesses that use a warehouse management system, the system typically generates replenishment movement transactions based on the inventory in the forward pick location. Many systems calculate a percent fill of the location and use a predefined trigger point to determine when replenishment should be done. It might be argued that the system should also examine open orders and replenish only when really necessary, but we are not aware of any commercial software that goes to that extent. A fixed trigger is probably sufficient for all practical purposes.

The objective of replenishment generation is to minimize the cost of replenishments. This is best done by maximizing the quantity replenished, which minimizes the number of times an item must be replenished. Since location capacity limits the replenishment quantity (to the capacity of the location less the on-hand quantity),

Best Practices in Replenishment

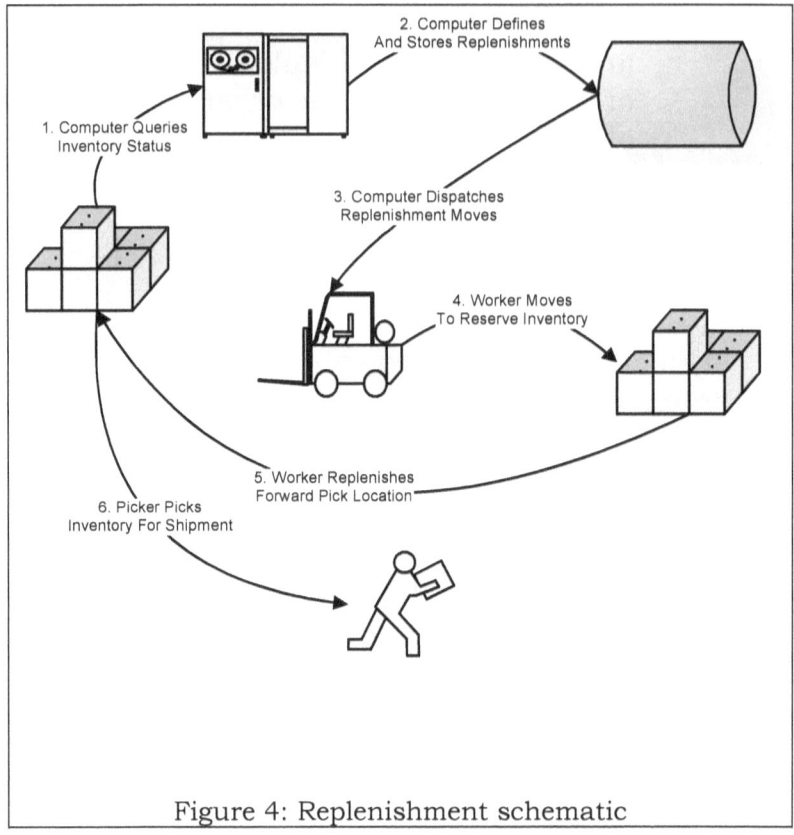

Figure 4: Replenishment schematic

the optimal strategy is to delay replenishment as long as possible.

Knowing how to set a replenishment trigger point is something of an art. Experience suggests:

1. Begin by estimating the time required to replenish a location. Take into consideration the distance to be traveled by the replenisher, the time

required to pick and put away the product, and the time that the generated replenishment will have to wait in queue before a person is assigned to it.

2. Then, for each product, calculate its usage over the estimated replenishment time. Set replenishment point at about 1.5 times usage for low variability products, 2 times usage for products with medium variability, and 3 times usage for highly volatile ones. Whether your replenishment trigger point is set as a percent fill of the forward pick location or as a quantity on hand is, of course, only a matter of arithmetic.

Manual Generation of Replenishments

Smaller warehouses and warehouses that operate without warehouse management systems may also want to take advantage of the benefits of replenishment and many do so successfully. The lack of a system that is capable of automatic replenishment generation, however, is a significant complication. We have seen two methods that can be successful, although they are both more error prone and less precise than the computer-driven approach.

Best Practices in Replenishment

The first approach is best used in warehouses that only need to replenish specific forward pick locations once or twice a week. A supervisor, controller, or possibly the replenishment operators themselves make a daily walkthrough of the forward pick area, examining stock levels, and listing the ones to be replenished. The actual replenishment work is then done either overnight or the next day. There will be products and pick locations missed and therefore the pickers will encounter unnecessary shortages. The process is labor intensive and does not work well in very large forward pick zones. But lacking a better way and assuming a measure of discipline, it can be sufficient.

Some warehouses depend on the pickers to manually identify the need for replenishment. Either the pickers are given voice radios or telephones are strategically placed throughout the forwards pick area. When the picker thinks that an item needs replenishment, he or she simply requests it. This process has obvious drawbacks. Although needed replenishments will be missed less often than with the supervisor's walkthrough, the pickers' desire to avoid stockouts and the extra work involved with them will often lead to too-frequent replenishment.

Best Practices in Replenishment

In either of these methods, or in almost any other imaginable manual method of triggering a replenishment move, a significant amount of human judgment is involved and the processes are thus almost certain to be less than optimal. However, in the event of need, they can work.

Operation and Control of Replenishments

Like all business processes, the monitoring and control of replenishment operations is as important as the proper design of the facilities and the methods.

Replenishment operators must be assigned in sufficient numbers to service needed work promptly, particularly in an environment where real-time processes generate replenishments and where replenishment trigger points are low. Obviously, if no one is available to do a replenishment, it won't get done.

The issue boils down to one of workload balancing so the replenishers on staff are capable of moving as much material into the forward pick area as the pickers are of moving it out. If there is a choice between having pickers wait for replenishment and having replenishers wait for work, the latter might be preferable.

Some warehouse management systems are capable of interleaving replenishments with other work (such as, possibly, putaways). These systems can offer significant advantage because they greatly simplify the workload balancing issue by

Best Practices in Replenishment

assuring that the replenishers do not run out of work. However, the system's interleaving scheme must define replenishment work as the top priority so the replenishers react to needs quickly and pickers don't run out of material.

Control implies measurement and a feedback loop that allows management to react to issues and correct imbalances before they become too serious. This paper suggests the following replenishment measures be made at least weekly – and preferably more often.

➢ Measure the number of replenishments generated (or executed) daily.

➢ List the items (possibly the top 50 and bottom 50) that are replenished most often and least often over a longer period, possibly a month. Both extremes represent items and locations that are candidates for review. They may need either location size adjustments and/or different positioning in the forward pick area.

➢ Log forward stockouts when they occur. For this purpose, a forward stockout is an initial bin visit in which the picker cannot immediately pick the quantity required, but for which there

Best Practices in Replenishment

is sufficient reserve stock. Ignore (for this purpose) whether or not the customer was actually served.

➢ List the items (the top 10 or 20) that were most frequently stocked out. Items that repetitively appear on this list are probably also candidates for review and investigation. They, also, may require larger or better placed forward pick locations or adjustments to their replenishment trigger points.

Direct Put-Away

Because replenishment contributes nothing directly to the serving of customer, it should be considered a necessary evil and as we should do as little of it as possible. One way to reduce the number of replenishments done is to use new receipts to fill up the forward picking location instead of putting them in reserve and then later moving them to forward picking.

However, direct putaway to forward picking is not always a good idea.

First, effectively accomplishing direct putaway almost always requires a real-time warehouse management system that can detect stock levels in forward picking and intelligently direct putaways in forward only when there is space to accomplish them. The waste associated with asking the putaway person to physically travel to forward picking when the location is actually full more than overcomes the savings.

Second, some warehouse layouts defeat the idea. The "flow-through" warehouse shown in Figure 5 is a good example. If the put-away operator has to travel through the reserve area to reach forward picking, then there is little value to direct put-away in forward. It may, in fact, be better to simply put everything in reserve and let the replenishers move it on to forward. (Of course there can be exceptions to this rule when out-of-stock product arrives.)

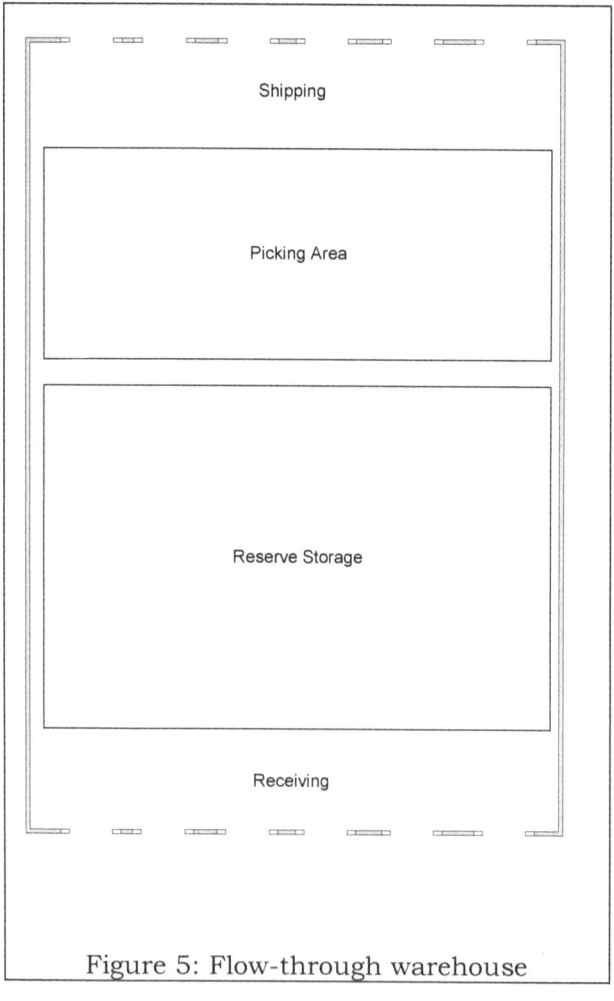

Figure 5: Flow-through warehouse

Best Practices in Replenishment

Even when it makes physical sense, direct putaway in forward picking may not be a good idea if stock rotation or product expiration is a concern. Conceivably, when a product is in frequent demand and arrives frequently in small quantities, a quantity could be stranded in reserve for a long time because customer needs are being met by new arrivals that travel directly from the receiving dock to forward picking. Some food and drug companies that deal with stringent product expiration rules still manage to successfully move product directly to forward picking, but they have to watch their product's age carefully and sometimes even have overrides that can prevent direct movement to forward picking when product in reserve is within a certain time of its expiration.

Finally, if you are interested in experimenting with direct put-away, be sure that your system has a threshold value so that the putaway operators aren't sent to forward picking if the pick location is full or if only a very small number of pieces can be stored there.

Replenishment With Highly Variable Demand

In some industries, demand is highly variable, to the extent that the optimum pick method can change from day to day or even from pick wave to pick wave. Some call these the "fashion" industries, but the term includes much more than apparel. Popular music and video distribution, toys and games and consumer electronics also experience surges in demand. Major recalls can have similar characteristics in the auto parts business. And there are other examples.

One approach to the management of highly variable demand has used the replenishment facilities built into most warehouse management systems. Firms have created a small group of forward pick locations specially equipped for very high volumes and have directed demand to these locations either automatically or manually (depending on the capabilities of their software) when the demand for a single item in a single day or a single wave exceeds a threshold value.

Redirecting demand creates picks for those locations. The replenishment algorithms, in turn, detect the need for product and plan movements of product into them. Some warehouse management systems are even able to control the quantities moved into the high volume pick locations so they do not exceed the demand quantity. When this is all done accurately, the result is that the pick locations are empty (or nearly empty) after the day or wave is complete, or after the decision is made to redirect demand back to the normal pick location.

These special, high-volume pick locations frequently consist of nothing more than a place to put two pallets on the floor, but sometimes include other facilities such as take-away conveyors, labeling equipment, or even scissor lifts to speed picking from pallets. The instances we are familiar with have dedicated only three or four such locations and less than a hundred square to this purpose with good effect. There are rarely more than three or four items that need this level of treatment at the same time.

All this amounts to a way of quickly and easily moving an item to a special pick location for a brief period of time. It can save significant amounts of work and the confusion that is always present when a pick location suddenly cannot be replenished fast enough and when pickers are getting in each other's way trying to reach it.

The downside of this method of handling highly variable demand is that it takes special software to accomplish it and either the software must automatically monitor demand or a human must do it.

Cascading Replenishment

One company in the mail order industry operated a high-rise, narrow aisle warehouse with relatively slow vehicles that could handle only pallets. Piece picking was done from a three-level mezzanine structure that was not accessible to the high-rise cranes, requiring a vehicle hand-off. This company installed extra rack between the high-rise area and forward picking and made it accessible to both the narrow aisle cranes and to conventional order picker vehicles. The space was called the "forward reserve" area. It was large enough to hold a single pallet of each SKU.

Pickers on the mezzanine would pick individual orders from carton flow rack, placing the merchandise in cartons that were then conveyed to a box sealer and manifesting station. A warehouse management system monitored flow rack inventories and when one dropped below a preset replenishment point, the system triggered replenishment from the forward reserve area. The replenishment move was done by the order picker vehicles and was also monitored by the warehouse management system. In turn, when stock in forward reserve reached its own replenishment

Best Practices in Replenishment

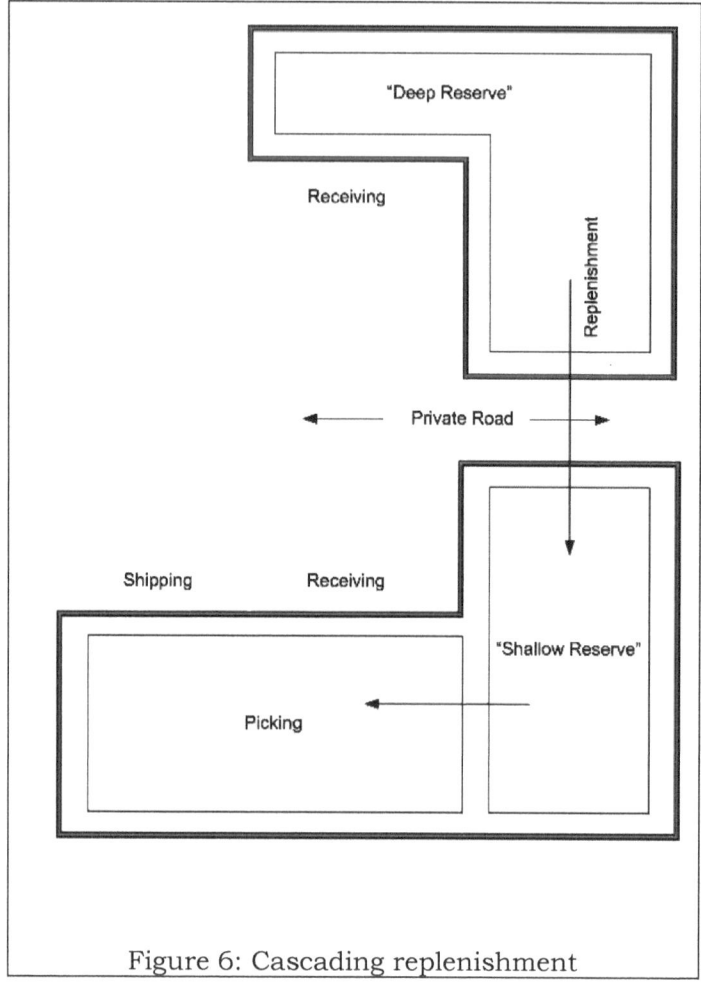

Figure 6: Cascading replenishment

point, the system triggered a secondary replenishment move of a pallet from high-rise reserve to forward reserve. The high-rise cranes of course, performed this secondary move.

Best Practices in Replenishment

The concept is called cascading replenishment, because a need in forward picking can create a need in the intermediate reserve area, which triggers a need for replenishment from bulk reserve.

A second company operated two buildings separated by a private roadway in a campus setting (see Figure 6). They used one building as "deep reserve" and did all picking in the other building. Partial pallet receipts were brought into the picking building and stored in "shallow reserve" for near-term use in the picking area, while full pallets were received in the deep reserve building and stored for eventual use. The pick lines were replenished from shallow reserve and shallow reserve was, in turn, replenished from deep reserve.

Cascading replenishment amounts to double handling of the product and thus is almost never a good thing by itself. These two examples, however, were driven by the necessities of the physical plant and their internal handling equipment. In both cases, cascading replenishment was made possible by the fact that the products being handled were not particularly age-sensitive and strict stock rotation was unnecessary. For them, the process worked. In most other instances, the practice is wasteful.

Best Practices in Replenishment

Summary

Replenishment adds no value to the product. It creates operational headaches when it doesn't happen on time and by subdividing warehouse space and creating additional labor classifications, it reduces space utilization and complicates work assignment. But when well done, can significantly reduce warehouse travel and thus increase productivity.

1. Replenishment should not be done as a knee-jerk reaction. It should be studied at an item-by-item level and should be done only when it pays for itself.

2. Forward picking locations should be sized appropriately to make replenishments as efficient as possible and to give the replenishers a reasonable chance to accomplish them on time.

3. Replenishment must be staffed adequately or work will pile up and pickers will encounter shortages.

4. The replenishment process requires study, engineering, and some level of experimentation before it will run smoothly

www.ingramcontent.com/pod-product-compliance
Lightning Source LLC
Chambersburg PA
CBHW021941170526
45157CB00005B/2378